TOM

The Voyage of the Dawn Treader

by

C. S. Lewis

Adapted by

Glyn Robbins

Samuel French – London
New York – Sydney – Toronto – Hollywood

ISBN 0 573 05085 6

THE VOYAGE OF THE DAWN TREADER

First performed at the Theatre Royal, Bath on September 9th, 1986. Subsequently on tour and at Sadler's Wells Theatre, London, with the following cast of characters:

Miraz	Yannis Lazarides
Bern	Andrew Jolly
Octesian	Tim Killick
Restimar	Robin Watson
Revilian	Alan Corser
Mavramorn	Sharon Lloyd
Argoz	Michael Bennett
Young Rhoop	Michael Howard
Edmund	Paul Ryan
Lucy	Tacye Lynette
Eustace	Kieron Smith
Caspian	Nicholas Farr
Drinian	Tim Killick
Rynelf	Robin Watson
Reepicheep	Franny O'Loughlin
Pug	Alan Corser
Tacks	Michael Howard
Gumpas	Yannis Lazarides
Soldier	Michael Bennett
Dragon	Michael Howard
Thumpers	Michael Bennett
	Alan Corser
	Michael Howard
	Sharon Lloyd
Aslan	Yannis Lazarides
Coriakin	Andrew Jolly
Rhoop	Andrew Jolly
Ramandu	Alan Corser
Ramandu's Daughter	Sharon Lloyd

The play directed by Richard Williams

Designed by Marty Flood

CHARACTERS

Miraz
Lord Bern
Lord Octesian
Lord Restimar
Lord Revilian
Lord Mavramorn
Lord Argoz
Lord Rhoop
Edmund
Lucy
Eustace
Prince Caspian, King of Narnia
Lord Drinian, Captain of the *Dawn Treader*
Rynelf, a crew member
Reepicheep, the most valiant mouse in the world
Pug, a slave-trader
Tacks, his henchman
Gumpas, Governor of the Lone Islands
Soldier
Dragon
Chief Thumper
Thumpers
Aslan, the Lion
Coriakin, the magician
Ramandu
Ramandu's Daughter

SYNOPSIS OF SCENES

Please note that the following billing should be used on all programmes and posters connected with performances of this play:

The Voyage of the Dawn Treader
by
C. S. Lewis
Adapted by Glyn Robbins

COVER ILLUSTRATION

The cover illustration for this play is reproduced by kind permission of the artist, Charles Jamieson, whose copyright it remains. Enquiries regarding the use of it, for whatever purpose, must be addressed to the artist c/o The Editorial Department, Samuel French Ltd.

PROLOGUE

Sounds of a crowd. As Miraz speaks, we see a tableau of the seven Lords who are about to set sail on the Eastern Ocean

Miraz People of Narnia. My people. We celebrate a happy day together today. I, Miraz, Lord Protector of our great land, caretaker of this fair and pleasant country—as long that is as Prince Caspian——

Lords Long live Prince Caspian!

Miraz —is still too young to be crowned as the true king—I, Miraz, your temporary ruler, have been persuaded by these seven of our noblest lords to allow them to sail away and look for new lands beyond—yes, beyond the Eastern Ocean. You may well gasp with astonishment. With amazement. Such bravery is far above and beyond the call of even Narnian duty. Where their quest will take them, nobody knows. What dangers await them, nobody knows. But we will hope and pray that they may find true glory and great treasures, and all sail back safely to us and to these shores. My people, may I present to you each one of these brave men. Men who alone in Narnia do not fear the sea. First, the Lord Bern. Well done, my brave Lord Bern. Now, Lord Octesian—a dragon of a man. My Lord, good luck. The Lord Restimar—if anyone can find gold, it's my Lord Restimar. Good hunting, my Lord. The Lord Revilian. The Lord Mavramorn. The Lord Argoz. And finally, the Lord Rhoop. Let us wish each lord in turn a fond farewell, a safe voyage and a speedy return. Farewell, dear Lords.

Lords Miraz, farewell!

Miraz Good fortune, dear Lords.

Lords Good fortune!

Miraz Safe return, dear Lords!

Lords Safe return. . . .

The seven Lords exit

Miraz (*to himself*) Preferably, in about a hundred years, my Lords. Well, now I've got rid of them, I can do what I like with Narnia.

Out of the dazzling sun comes the roar of a great lion

ACT I

SCENE 1

A bedroom

Edmund and Lucy are discovered sitting, looking at a picture of a dragon-ship on the wall US

Lucy It's a beautiful picture, Edmund. It looks like a real dragon-ship.

Edmund Running before a fast wind, heading off to adventure and glory, I'll be bound. Not like being stuck here for the holidays. In this dreadful house. With our dreadful uncle and our even more dreadful aunt. And that entirely dreadful cousin, Eustace. Eustace Clarence Scrubbs. What a name! It suits him perfectly.

Lucy Such a very Narnian ship.

There is a pause

Edmund Oh, Lucy, don't you just long to go back to Narnia?

Lucy (*dreamily*) The land behind the wardrobe. Oh, I miss Narnia so much ...

Edmund And Aslan?

Lucy And Aslan most of all.

Edmund The question is, does it make things worse, having to look at a Narnian ship when you can't do anything about it, or ...?

Lucy Or is even just looking at it better than doing nothing at all. What was it we were told? "Don't try to get back to Narnia, it'll happen when you least expect it."

Eustace, who has been listening, enters

Eustace
    "Some kids who played games about Narnia
    Got gradually barmier and barmier
    Then one fine day, they were taken away
    And locked up in the looney-bin."

How about that, then?

Edmund It doesn't rhyme, Eustace.

Eustace It doesn't matter, Edmund. All you two have done since you came here to stay is talk about Narnia. Fine cousins you are—no fun at all. What is this soppy Narnia, anyway?

Lucy Well, it's a whole land full of wonderful people: lions, leopards, dwarfs, fauns, satyrs, cats, dogs and mice.

Edmund And don't forget the beavers, and Aslan.

Eustace Where is this wonderful land of yours then? I don't exactly remember it from geography lessons.

Edmund They don't teach it in geography, stupid.

Lucy You won't find it in any atlas.

Eustace Well, how did you get there, then?

Edmund He won't believe you, Lucy.

Lucy We found it at the back of our wardrobe.

Eustace (*laughing*) At the back of your wardrobe. Don't be ridiculous. Whoever heard of a country at the back of a wardrobe?

Edmund (*thoughtfully*) That's what I said once.

Eustace (*scornfully*) Narnia, indeed. And who or what is Aslan, when he's at home to tea? You two made it all up. It's a pack of lies.

Lucy But Aslan is the——

Edmund Don't say anything, Lucy, and perhaps the little stinker will go away.

Eustace I live here, you don't. You can go away, Edmund. And good riddance. (*With a change of voice*) Do you like that picture, Lucy?

Lucy Yes, I do, Eustace. It's a most beautiful dragon-ship.

Eustace No, it isn't, Lucy. It's a rotten ship. A stupid ship. And anyway, dragons don't exist and never have. Ma and Pa said so. So it must be true.

Edmund Well, if you leave the room, you won't have to look at it, will you?

As they turn away, the picture begins to enlarge

Eustace This is my house. I do the ordering about around here. It's about time you two so-called guests realized that. What's so special about the mouldy old picture, anyway? I'll just take it down and throw it away. That'll show you.

Lucy You can't, you can't.

Eustace I can. Dreadful, am I? "Dreadful uncle, and our even more dreadful aunt, and that entirely dreadful cousin." Dreadful, eh? I'll show you just how dreadful I can be ...

They turn back

Edmund Hold on you two, something's happening. Hold on!

Lucy Oh, look! Just look! The picture's getting bigger. The water looks really wet! The waves are going up and down!

Eustace They can't be! They can't be! Ouch! That's salt water!

Edmund The ship's moving. And it's getting bigger and bigger.

Which it is and, as the Children stare open-mouthed, the picture comes to life

Lucy The picture's coming to life.

Eustace runs towards it

Eustace Stop it! It's a trick! Stop it! It can't come to life. It's not allowed! I'll smash it! I'll smash it to bits.

Lucy Stop him, Edmund.

Lucy and Edmund try to stop Eustace. As they struggle, the picture grows bigger and bigger, the sound of waves, wind and gulls fills the theatre, the Lights dim, and the Children fall into the sea

Eustace Let me go, Edmund. It's a dream. It's something I ate. It's just a bad dream. No, it isn't. It's a nightmare. Look at the dragon. Look at the dragon's head. It's real. I'm falling. I'm falling.
Edmund Me too. I'm falling as well.
Lucy We're all falling into the sea ... Swim! Swim for your lives!
Edmund Kick off your shoes! Kick off your shoes!
Eustace I'm drowning. I'm drowning.
Lucy Grab the ropes! Grab the ropes!
Eustace Save me! Save me!

SCENE 2

The Dawn Treader *at sea*

The Children are hauled on board to face a golden-haired young man, Caspian, aged about eighteen; an older man, Drinian; and Rynelf. Standing apart from all of them, slightly hidden, is Reepicheep

Lucy (*shivering*) Ca-Ca-Caspian!
Edmund (*the same*) C-C-Caspian, K-King of N-Narnia!
Caspian Well met, my friends.
Edmund W-w-well m-met ind-deed.
Eustace It isn't well met at all. I could have been drowned.
Caspian Drinian, spiced wine for our guests, they need something to warm them after their swim.
Drinian Ay ay, Sire. Rynelf! Get below and aft to the galley.
Rynelf Below'n'afterthegally, Cap'n?
Caspian (*explaining*) Under the deck to the kitchen, Rynelf.
Rynelf Thank you, Sire.

Rynelf disappears below deck

Caspian He's a brave man, but he's never been to sea before.
Drinian (*half-aside*) Landlubber!
Caspian Control yourself, Drinian. (*To the Children*) Who is your companion?
Eustace M-mind your own business. And don't touch me. I'm wet and cold and I want to go home. Let me go at once.
Caspian Let you go? (*He looks around*) But, to where?

Rynelf enters with a steaming flagon of wine which he pours into silver cups and passes round

May I propose a toast? Welcome aboard the *Dawn Treader*.

All except Eustace: "The Dawn Treader!" *Eustace has not waited for the toast. He drinks, turns green and rushes to the side of the ship*

Eustace Oh! Ooh! Ooooergh!

Reepicheep, standing beside him, laughs

Reepicheep That's a merry shipmate you've brought us, Majesties. Not a good sailor, I fear.

Eustace Ugh! Ugh! What's that! Take it away, it's horrid.

Lucy throws open her arms, then changes her mind and folds them

Lucy (*with great affection*) Oh, Reepicheep.

Reepicheep makes a knee, kisses Lucy's hand, straightens up and twirls 'his whiskers

Reepicheep My humble duty to your Majesty. To both your Majesties. Nothing excepting your Majesties' presence was lacking to this great adventure.

Eustace Majesties? Where? What majesties?

Lucy Us, Eustace. Edmund and I. We were Kings and Queens of Narnia, once.

Edmund And once a king or queen of Narnia, always a king or queen of Narnia.

Eustace What rubbish!

Edmund Good to see you, Reep. You look fighting fit.

Lucy Sir Reepicheep—the bravest fighting mouse in all the world.

Eustace Fighting mouse, indeed! I hate mice. And I hate performing animals even more. They're silly, vulgar and sentimental. Ma and Pa say so. So it must be true. Take it away, somebody.

Reepicheep stares at Eustace, then turns to Lucy

Reepicheep Am I to understand that this singularly discourteous person is under your Majesties' protection? Because, if not . . . (*He places his paw on the sword hilt threateningly*)

Lucy and Edmund sneeze

Caspian Forgive me, friends. I'm a fool to keep you standing here in your wet clothes. Reepicheep, Drinian, find warm blankets for their Majesties and their friend.

Drinian At once, Sire. Rynelf, you'll find blankets below and aft in my sea-chest. Got it?

Rynelf Yes, Cap'n.

Drinian Ay ay, Cap'n.

Rynelf Yes—er—ay ay, Cap'n.

Rynelf goes below deck

Drinian He'll need a hand, Reep.

Reepicheep To the comfort of a lady, even honour must sometimes give way—(*to Eustace*) for the moment.

Reepicheep exits

Edmund (*to Caspian*) But what are you all doing here?
Eustace I'm getting colder.
Lucy How long has it been?
Eustace And feeling sick again.
Edmund Where are you all going?
Eustace I bet I've got flu.
Lucy When did we last see each other?
Eustace And pneumonia.
Edmund What is this wonderful ship?
Eustace I'll have to go to the nearest hospital.

Lucy			Caspian, where are we going?
Eustace	} (*together*)	{	I ask you, where are we going?
Edmund			Caspian, where are we going?

Caspian (*laughing*) Wait! Wait! Give me a chance!

Reepicheep and Rynelf enter with blankets and give them to the Children.
Rynelf takes up a position as look-out

First, may I present to you properly my Captain, the Lord Drinian. Now we—this lovely ship, which is called the *Dawn Treader*, the Captain here, Reepicheep, Rynelf and I are on an expedition.
Edmund Off to find adventure and glory?
Reepicheep Precisely, your Majesty.
Caspian Perhaps you remember being told that when I was an orphan child my wicked Uncle Miraz stole the throne from me? And that he sent seven of my father's friends to explore the Eastern Seas beyond the Lone Islands . . .?
Edmund Seven Lords. I remember. And they never came back, did they?
Caspian Exactly as my wicked uncle had intended.
Lucy And at your coronation——
Caspian —I swore an oath to sail east for a year and a day to find my father's missing friends—or to learn at least what had happened to them.
Lucy But who's in charge of Narnia, while you're away?
Caspian Why, Trumpkin the Dwarf, of course. An excellent regent, eh Drinian?
Drinian Loyal as a badger, and valiant as a lion——
Reepicheep Ahem!
Drinian —er, as a mouse, my King.
Lucy And have you yet learnt what happened to the seven men?
Caspian The seven Narnian Lords who alone did not fear the sea. No, not yet. They were sent to look for new lands beyond the Eastern Ocean. Strange stories have been heard. Tales of a string of islands that lead eventually to a great sea-wave . . .
Drinian Tales of a huge comber that sucks unwary ships off the edge of the world and sends them back to the beginning of time. Tales of deadly dragons, of invisible beings, of slave-traders, of mermaids and mermen that can sing a sailor into the sea to his inevitable watery death . . .
Caspian Tales of treasure. Tales of so much gold that it would make Narnia

the most powerful nation in the world. And its king would be so rich——

Reepicheep Ahem.

Caspian Oh yes, we should also, of course, explain that the valiant Reepicheep has a higher purpose. Reep, would you care to explain?

Reepicheep When I learnt that Prince Caspian was to fulfil his coronation promise and look for the missing Lords, I realized that the journey might take us to the eastern end of the world. And I thought, what might we find there?

Eustace But there isn't an end to the world. Everyone knows that. The world is round, you silly mouse.

Reepicheep makes to draw

Edmund Our world may well be round, however ... Narnia is most certainly different. Narnian time, for example, is totally different from our time. A hundred Narnian years is the blink of an eye to us.

Eustace A blink of an eye indeed ...

Edmund Pray continue, most valiant Reepicheep.

Eustace Oh, valiant is it?

Edmund And Eustace ...

Eustace Yes?

Edmund Shut up! (*He hits him*)

Reepicheep I intend to find the end of the world, where, I believe, lies the country of Aslan. When I was in my cradle, a prophecy was made:

> "Where sky and water meet,
> Where the waves grow sweet,
> Doubt not, Reepicheep,
> That you will find all you seek.
> For there is the utter East."

I have known all my life that I must seek out the utter East. And I have known that I must seek out Aslan. Though why, in truth, I cannot tell.

Lucy And Aslan always comes from the East—of course.

Eustace But who or what is Aslan?

Reepicheep (*to Lucy*) As always, your Majesty understands me perfectly.

Drinian Get forrard, Rynelf!

Rynelf Ay ay, Cap'n. But where is "forrard", Captain?

Drinian Get to the front, man. To the pointed end.

Rynelf Ay ay, Cap'n.

Edmund And where are we now, Captain Drinian?

Drinian Near the Lone Islands, Majesty. We have been now nearly thirty days at sea and sailed more than four hundred leagues from the mainland of Narnia.

Edmund And beyond the Lone Islands?

Drinian Nobody knows, your Majesty. Unless the Lone Islanders can tell us.

Eustace I'm feeling sick again. I want to be put ashore. I'll find the British Consul and get sent home. And this time, I'll travel by air. I can't stand ships. And I'll lodge a disposition against you all.

Reepicheep A disposition? Is that a new form of fight? Of single combat, perhaps?

Eustace (*finally losing control*) You really are a stupid little mouse. Everyone knows what a disposition is. Go away from me.

He pushes Reepicheep, who stumbles backwards and falls

I've a good mind to pick you up by your feet and whirl you round my head until you get some sense into your tiny little pea-brain.

As Eustace bends down, Reepicheep draws his sword and pricks Eustace twice. Eustace, squealing, lets him go

Reepicheep Draw, you poltroon. Draw and fight, or I'll beat you black and blue with the flat of my sword blade.

Rynelf Land! Land right in front of us.

Drinian Rynelf! Say it properly! Land ho! Land dead ahead!

Rynelf Ay ay, Cap'n. Land ho! Land dead ahead!

Drinian (*to Caspian*) Land dead ahead, Sire.

Caspian What land, Captain?

Drinian What do you see, look-out?

Rynelf An island. It looks sort of bluey-green; or greeny-blue, if you know what I mean.

Drinian Hopeless. (*To Caspian*) We've reached the Lone Islands, Sire. The look-out reports "a sort of bluey-green or greeny-blue if you know what I mean", Sire.

Caspian I do exactly. Isn't that the island of Felimath?

Lucy Which if I remember right is inhabited.

Edmund And if I remember right, it belongs to the true King of Narnia.

Caspian I wonder if the inhabitants know that I am the new true King? Drinian, we'll anchor *Dawn Treader* away from towns or villages and row ashore and take a look at Felimath.

Drinian Ay ay, Sire. Rynelf, make ready to anchor.

Rynelf Ay ay, Captain.

Caspian Perhaps we will find some of my Lords here.

Drinian Perhaps . . .

Black-out

SCENE 3

Pug, a slave-trader, enters with Tacks, his henchman, who is carrying a whip

Pug I tell yer, Tacks, life is gettin' 'arder.

Tacks Ar.

Pug It's gettin' so 'ard, I don't know as it's worth livin' 'ere any more. I fink we'll 'ave ter move.

Tacks Ar.

Pug We are runnin' out of livestock an' that's the truth.

Tacks Ar.

Pug Our 'ole economy, our 'ole prosperity, our 'ole future is built on buyin' an' sellin' slaves.

Tacks Ar.

Pug An' there ain't no more slaves.

Tacks Ar.

Pug The facks is, we've run out. We just simply run out of slaves. I am at the end of my tether.

Tacks Ar.

Pug A lifetime of civilized slave-tradin' slippin' slowly to its unwarranted an' un'appy end. It will be a great sadness, a great loss to the community at large.

Eustace (*off*) At last! Safe! On dry land! Now where's the British Consul?

Pug Whassat? Take cover.

Tacks Ar?

Pug (*hitting him*) 'Ide, yer fool!

They hide behind some bushes

Lucy and Eustace enter R

Eustace I don't care what you say, Lucy, I'm going straight to the authorities whoever they are, wherever we are . . .

Lucy But Eustace, you don't understand . . .

Eustace And don't think a stupid girl is going to stop me. Ma and Pa——

Pug and Tacks come out of their hide-out and capture the Children. Tacks bundles them off stage L. *During the following Tacks enters*

Pug In the cage with 'em, Tacks. Don't forget ter gag 'em. Fings is beginnin'—just beginnin', mind yer—ter look up.

Tacks Ar.

Edmund (*off*) Which island is this, Reep?

Reepicheep (*off*) The island of Felimath.

Pug Just beginnin', mind yer. Get down, Tacks.

Tacks Ar . . .

They hide

Edmund and Reepicheep enter

Reepicheep The island of Felimath, Sire. I heard a tale once—though I can hardly believe it true—that the natives still practise slave-trading.

Edmund What? Buying and selling people?

Reepicheep And animals as well. For gold. Unbelievable, isn't it?

Edmund Where are Lucy and Eustace?

Reepicheep They must have run on ahead——

Edmund and Reepicheep are captured

Tacks carries them off

Pug Don't forget ter tie them tight an' gag 'em 'ard, Tacks.
Tacks (*off*) Ar.
Caspian (*off*) Edmund! Reepicheep! Wait for me.

Tacks enters

Pug Fings is beginning to look very good indeed. Down, Tacks.
Tacks Ar.

They hide

Caspian enters

Caspian Where are you all? Don't you know it's dangerous to split up on an unknown island. Our strength lies in——

After a short fight, Caspian is captured and gagged

Pug Five is a goodly number, Tacks. I'll shut his mouth, while you get the others.

Tacks goes to get the prisoners and whips them on stage

Take the skin off their backs, Tacks.

The prisoners, tied and gagged, are lined up together

Right you lot. You are now my prisoners. You are in fact very lucky people. Not for you the ugly death you might've 'ad if we'd been cannibals. Not for you the disfigurement or death you might've 'ad if we'd been enemy soldiers. Oh, no, no, no. None of that plank walkin' what pirates might've made yer do. No salt mines, no rowin' in the galleys, no 'ard labour camps. You 'ave been very lucky. You 'ave fallen on your feet and into the right 'ands. You are goin' to be taken to the finest slave market——

All Slave market!
Pug —the finest slave market in the world, and sold to the 'ighest bidder and may I tell you——

Lord Bern enters

But why me? His Lordship here will tell you that Lone Island slaves are sought arter by the 'ole world, and so given only the best treatment. Eh, my Lord?
Bern At it again, Pug? You despicable man! Slave-trading! Traffic in human beings. Buying and selling bodies and minds. The most disgusting business in the world. The slaves here are sought after because it's the last place in all Narnia that practises the evil trade. I just wish Caspian, the new King of Narnia, knew about it. And were here to do something about it.
Pug 'Ardly likely, Sir. 'Ardly likely. With 'im so far away. Anyway, 'e'd proberly turn a blind eye, Sir. Like 'is uncle, the king before 'im. 'Is governor gets a percentage, arter all. So why shouldn't the new king? Now, do you want to buy—or are you still penniless, my Lord?

Bern I'd buy them all from you if I could, you foul apology for a man. I have a few coins. Will these buy freedom for one of the poor wretches?

Pug Just the one, my Lord.

Eustace pushes forward. Bern selects Caspian

Bern Let it be this one, then. (*To the others*) If I could help you, strangers, I would. But I am now completely penniless.

Pug sneers and drags off the slave train

Pug Now, little piggies, let's go to market.

All exit except Caspian and Lord Bern

Lord Bern makes to exit

Caspian You're a penniless lord?

Bern There are a few, you know. Buying you has cost me my food for a week. I'm afraid it'll be a hungry sort of freedom for you, my friend.

Caspian My Lord, do you have a name?

Bern I was known as the Lord Bern.

Caspian But I have been looking for you, my Lord. You are my father's friend!

Bern Father? What father?

Caspian I am Caspian, King of Narnia, son of Caspian the lawful King of Narnia, Lord of Cair Paravel, and Emperor of the Lone Islands.

Bern By Aslan, it is his father's very voice and trick of speech. You have his looks, his voice, his style, his authority. Yes, I believe you, slave. You are indeed my liege Lord, Majesty. (*He kneels and kisses Caspian's hand*)

Caspian pulls him to his feet

Caspian How are you here?

Bern I came at the "request" of your uncle, Miraz, with my six companions in search of land and treasure. We anchored here. I fell in love with the island and felt I had had enough of the sea. I knew that your Majesty's uncle hated me, so rather than go back, I have lived here ever since.

Caspian And the others?

Bern They sailed onwards. But what of your friends?

Caspian Where will they be taken?

Bern To the slave auction held here by your usurping uncle's royal decree. The money made from the sale of slaves goes straight into the pockets of Gumpas.

Caspian Who is Gumpas?

Bern Governor Gumpas. The cruel and corrupt ruler of these islands who was appointed by your uncle, King Miraz. Have you any money, Sire, to buy freedom for your friends? I, Majesty, have none.

Caspian I came here with one ship and a small crew. I did not expect to have to barter for the freedom of slaves. I have no money with me, but by the might of Aslan I will speak with this man, Gumpas! There will be no slavery anywhere in Narnia as long as I am king! Lord Bern, you must go at once to my ship, the *Dawn Treader* and fetch my captain, Drinian, and his crewman, Rynelf. Bring them to the slave auction. I will meet you there.

Bern These are brave words . . . as indeed befits a king of Narnia. But I fear that Gumpas is bound to have you killed, if you go there alone.

Caspian Then what is to be done?

Bern There may be a way. You say you have just the one ship.

Caspian Yes. The *Dawn Treader*.

Bern But if Gumpas were to think you had a large fleet standing by . . .

Caspian Yes?

Bern Go alone to the slave auction. But take this horn with you. I will arrange with all the captains of all the ships lying in the harbour that at the sound of that horn they and their crews will create such a hullabaloo that Gumpas will think he's been invaded by the whole of Narnia!!

Caspian An excellent idea! Go quickly, Lord Bern, you have a great deal to do. I will see you at the slave market.

Caspian exits

Bern Be careful, Sire.

Lord Bern exits

Pug, Gumpas, Governor of the Lone Islands, and a Soldier enter

Pug Life, Governor Gumpas, is getting 'arder.

Gumpas So, 'ard, hard, I mean, that it's not worth living here any more. Yes, Pug, I've heard it all before.

Pug 'Owever, Governor Gumpas, Sir.

Gumpas Yes, Pug.

Pug By a stroke of luck or is it genius, Sir, I 'ave managed to collect no less than four objects for your perusal.

Gumpas FOUR SLAVES?

Caspian appears behind the Soldier

Pug Yes, Sir.

Gumpas That's amazing, Pug. That's very good news indeed.

Pug Thank yer, Sir.

Caspian disarms the Soldier and drags him off

It 'as not been easy. And I 'ope you will—well—recognize that, Sir.

Caspian reappears, disguised as the Soldier

Gumpas Of course, Pug, of course. In the usual way. The usual percentage. We'll ring the slave bell straightaway, then. Soldier, go, bring my chair and command that the slave bell be rung.

Caspian Yes, Governor, Sir.

Caspian exits

Gumpas Pug, bring them in.

Pug beckons to Tacks who is waiting with the prisoners off

> *The slave train comes on, and a bell begins to toll. Caspian returns with a chair for Gumpas*

Tacks, bring them forward. For inspection.

Tacks pushes Eustace forward

Eustace Eustace Clarence Scrubbs, at your service.

Gumpas What a silly name. (*He tweaks Eustace's nose and moves to Reepicheep*) This one can go straight to the circus. (*He moves to Lucy*) And this one can go straight to the kitchens. (*He moves to Edmund*) This one is a particularly fine specimen. By the authority invested in me as Governor of the Lone Islands by the King of Narnia, I declare this slave auction may commence. (*He sits*) Pug, pray continue.

Pug Governor Gumpas, ladies, gentlemen. I 'ave 'ere a rare and choice selection of the finest goods, newly arrived on our shores, for your delectation, appreciation and eventual purchase. Lot number one. (*He indicates Edmund*) A fine agricultural labourer, suitable for 'ard work in the fields, the mines or the galleys.

Lucy But you told us that——

Pug Tacks.

Tacks Ar. (*He whips Lucy silent*)

Reepicheep Coward!

Pug As I was saying, ladies and gents, suitable for the fields, mines or the galleys. Under twenty-one. Not a bad tooth in his 'ead. Good strong fellow. Look at 'is muscles. What am I bid? Ten crescents. You must be joking! Over there—fifteen? There, eighteen. Twenty-one. Twenty-three. Twenty-four crescents. Going once. Twice. And sold, to the gentleman on the right.

Gumpas Twenty-four crescents. Fifteen per cent to me. That's twenty-four times fifteen over a hundred, equals three point sixty crescents due to me. Right, Pug?

Pug Yes, Governor Sir. And now, ladies and gentlemen, lot two. (*He indicates Lucy and Eustace*) An unusual lot this one: a matched pair. Very unusual, a bit scrawny, but capable of fattenin'. Personally, I would use them as 'ouse slaves for a few years to build them up, and then turn them over to 'arder labour.

Lucy But you said——

Tacks whips her again

Oh, Aslan! Aslan! Please help us!

Caspian who has been standing behind Gumpas' chair, snatches the whip from Tacks and sends him flying

Caspian Slaver, you have sold your last human being.

Gumpas Pug! Get rid of him . . .

A fight. Caspian battles with Pug, Tacks, Gumpas and releases Reepicheep. As all seems about to be lost, Caspian blows the horn. Sounds of answering horns, cheering, firecrackers, etc.

Lord Bern, Rynelf and Drinian enter

Bern On your knees, every man jack of you. On your knees to the King of Narnia.

Gumpas Who?

Caspian Slave-trader, your life is forfeit.

Pug Why Sir?

Caspian Because I abolished the foul and inhuman practice of slave-trading on the islands half an hour ago. On pain of instant death.

Pug But I didn't know, Sir.

Caspian Ignorance of the law is no excuse, slaver. On your knees and beg for mercy.

Bern Every slave in this market is free.

Cheers. Rynelf and Drinian untie the slaves and remove the chair

Caspian By my royal decree.

Gumpas Your Majesty, I must protest.

Caspian Tell me, Governor Gumpas, what need do we have for slaves, Governor?

Gumpas To sell them for export. The Lone Islands are a centre, a major centre for exporting slaves.

Bern Rubbish! You sell slaves in order to put money——

Gumpas Be silent, Lord Bern.

Bern —into Pug's pockets and to put money into your own private accounts.

Gumpas I protest, Sire. I have documents, statistics, accounts, books and diagrams that prove——

Caspian That show how you exchange slaves for food, grain, wine, timber for the benefit of the people of the islands?

Gumpas Well no, Sir, not exactly Sir.

Caspian Well no, Sir, not at all, Sir. The traffic in slaves is abolished. And so, Governor Gumpas, are you.

Gumpas I beg your Majesty's pardon?

Caspian My royal decree is that the Lord Bern is the new Governor—no— is now Duke of all the Lone Islands and rules on my behalf until I or my successor command differently. The island is free.

All cheer

Bern Majesty, you do me great honour.

Caspian No more than you deserve. I suggest, Bern, that you put the slaver and his henchman to some useful civic work like mending the roads. Gumpas might make a useful roadmender, too.

Bern Your Majesty, I will certainly deal with these three.

Caspian As you wish, Lord Bern.

Bern Perhaps a short spell in prison might help them decide how best they can help the island. Rynelf, take them away.

Rynelf, Gumpas, Pug and Tacks exit

Bern Sire, will you stay for a small feast of celebration?
Caspian No, Lord Bern. We must venture on, in the name of Aslan, to find your companions in the East.
Reepicheep The East, the utter East.

Wind stirs

Caspian Captain Drinian, have you made enquiries of the islanders?
Drinian We all have, Sire. They know nothing of any lands beyond the islands. Only a legend of a huge wave that sweeps everything it catches over the edge of the world.
Reepicheep So this is where true adventure really starts!

The wind is rising

Caspian Govern well, Lord Bern. Pray to Aslan for our safe return.
Bern Farewell, my King, I hope you find my six companions well and alive. Farewell.
All Farewell.

They exit

The stage darkens as the wind rises to a full hurricane. Out of the darkness emerges a storm-tattered Dawn Treader

SCENE 4

A storm at sea

Drinian, Rynelf and Caspian are on deck. During a lull, Lucy and Edmund appear

Drinian GET BELOW, SIRE. GET BELOW, MA'AM. Take the helm, Prince Caspian. I must get forrard. (*He moves forward towards the prow*)
Lucy We've been below for thirteen days.
Edmund It's foul below. We need fresh air.
Drinian It's foul up here, too. Get below, your Majesties.
Edmund Captain, the food has run out. The water casks are shattered. We must find land or turn back.
Drinian We have run before this gale for eighteen days. We have no maps, no way of knowing where land might be. We cannot turn back against this wind, Sire.
Lucy What can we do?
Drinian Get below, your Majesties, and pray for help from Aslan.

Edmund We've been doing that already.

Rynelf Land ho! Land to the right of us! And to the left! A rocky shore! Horror! Steep cliffs and breakers! We're too close!

Drinian Hard aport, Caspian. Put the rudder hard aport!

Rynelf Rocks dead ahead. Watch out or we'll wreck.

Drinian Come round, in Aslan's name. Come round *Dawn Treader*. COME ROUND. ASLAN! SAVE OUR SOULS!

A splintering noise, and the stage darkens

Scene 5

Dragon Island

Eustace enters

Eustace First, a picture comes to life. Then, I'm half-drowned. Then I'm dragged on board that horrible ship to meet a bunch of real weirdos. I get attacked by a mouse. Then I'm sold as a slave. And finally shipwrecked on this awful looking island. Well, one thing's for sure, I'm never going back on the *Dawn Treader* again. Never, ever again. I hope it's so badly damaged that it never puts to sea again. There must be a British Consul somewhere. There's always a British Consul. Whenever you're in trouble abroad, go to the British Consul. That's what Ma and Pa say. So it must be true. And what about that dreadful storm? I hate the sea. I'd much rather fly. I love flying. It's much safer. And quicker. Why, the crew of that awful ship hadn't even got emergency rockets or a radio to call for help. All they did was yell for Aslan, whatever that may mean. Aslan! Aslan! What a silly name! But at least I've got away from that nasty little mouse. He really hurt me with that spiky little sword of his. Ooh, I can still feel it. I detest that Reepicheep. He's not a mouse, he's a rat. A rotten little rat. Oh, where's this British Consul? What's that over there? It looks like smoke. And where there's smoke, there's fire. That's what Ma and Pa always say. A nice, warm fire to dry me out. And I won't tell the others.

The smoke is coming from a cave US, *towards which he walks*

(*He stumbles*) What's that? (*He bends down, picks something up and rubs it*) It's a coin. A gold coin. Gold! There's some more! Yes, look. Here. And here. And here. And those look like jewels. Look at this beautiful armlet. (*He picks the armlet up and wears it*) Why, the cave is full of treasure. I've found a treasure cave! And finders keepers. It's mine, all mine. Now I'll show everyone who's really in charge. What's that? Ugh! That's disgusting . . .

Eustace disappears into the cave

Caspian, Lucy, Edmund, Drinian, and Reepicheep enter. Edmund is now carrying a sword

All Eustace! Eustace!

Caspian (*shouting*) EUSTACE! Surely he must hear that, wherever he is.

Lucy (*calling*) Eustace! Eustace, where are you? The ship's repaired. We're ready to sail, now.

Edmund Typical Eustace. I bet he's looking for a British Consul. Good riddance to him.

Lucy We must do something. He may have got lost or fallen into a hole . . .

Drinian Or been captured by savages . . .

Caspian Or killed by wild beasts . . .

Lucy Or eaten by cannibals . . .

Edmund In whichever case, as I said, good riddance to bad rubbish.

Reepicheep You never spoke a word that became you less, Sire. Eustace is certainly no friend of mine, but while he is one of our fellowship, it behoves our honour to find him, or to avenge him if he is dead.

Caspian (*wearily*) Yes, you're absolutely right, Reepicheep, of course we have to find him.

Edmund (*sotto voce*) If we can.

Caspian It's just the nuisance of it. It means a search party and endless trouble. Bother Eustace!

Drinian With the greatest respect, Sire, we must decide what to do, now. It is getting dark—and will soon be nightfall. We will need shelter, food and a warm fire.

Caspian You're suggesting we should give up the search for the night, Drinian?

Drinian Yes, Sire.

Reepicheep Surely, my King, we must of honour's sake continue until it is dark, and worry about our personal comfort after that.

Lucy He might be hurt. Every minute could count.

Edmund But there is shelter, and what looks like fire. (*He points to the cave*)

Lucy A cave. Smoke. Where there's smoke, there's almost always fire.

Reepicheep and Edmund approach the cave

Drinian I counsel that we spend the night here in safety, and continue the search tomorr—— What's the matter?

Reepicheep and Edmund start to back away from the cave as twin jets of smoke belch out at them

Lucy What is it?

Caspian I know exactly what it is . . .

Drinian What, Sire?

Caspian Scatter everyone! Scatter and hide!

The Dragon roars

Edmund It's a dragon! Run everyone!

They scatter and hide, except for Reepicheep

Caspian Reepicheep, you will not fight that dragon.

Reepicheep But Sire, honour commands——
Caspian Get back, I say. And that is a *royal* command.

The Dragon roars. Reepicheep reluctantly retreats

   The Dragon comes out of the cave, limping

Edmund Why is it wagging its head like that?
Caspian And nodding?
Lucy And limping?
Drinian There's something coming from its eyes.
Lucy Oh, can't you see? It's crying. Those are tears.
Drinian I shouldn't trust to that, Ma'am. That's what crocodiles do. To put you off guard.
Edmund It wagged its head when you said that, as if it was trying to say "No".
Lucy Do you think it understands what we are saying?

The Dragon nods

Reepicheep Dragon, can you understand speech?

The Dragon nods

Reepicheep Can you speak?

The Dragon shakes its head

Reepicheep If you come in friendship, dragon, raise your left foreleg above your head.

The Dragon raises its left foreleg, and cries in pain. The leg is obviously swollen around a too-tight armlet

Lucy Oh look, there's something wrong with its leg. It needs help.
Drinian Be careful, Queen Lucy. It might be a trick.
Lucy Show me your leg, poor dragon. I might be able to help. Fetch water, someone, please.

All crowd around

Caspian Look!
Edmund Look at what?
Caspian Look at the armlet.
Reepicheep Look at the device on the armlet: a hammer with a diamond above it. The sign of a great Narnian lord.
Caspian The Lord Octesian!
Lucy Perhaps this is the Lord Octesian turned into a dragon.

The Dragon shakes its head

Drinian Or perhaps this dragon has devoured the Lord Octesian.

The Dragon shakes its head violently

Edmund Are you the Lord Octesian?

The Dragon shakes its head

Lucy Are you someone enchanted? Someone human?

The Dragon nods

Edmund You're not ...
Lucy You couldn't be——
Reepicheep —Eustace, by any chance?

The Dragon nods violently and cries loudly

Edmund How did it happen?

The Dragon shakes its head sadly

Caspian We'll talk all about that in the morning. Night is falling and it's getting very dark. Now we've found him, and found shelter and warmth, what we all need most of all is a good night's sleep. Can we get you anything in the meantime, Eustace?

The Dragon nods

Drinian Food?

The Dragon shakes its head

Lucy Water? You must be very thirsty.

The Dragon nods. Drinian fetches water and gives it to the Dragon. The water turns to steam. The Dragon cries

Lucy The dragon just turns the water to steam.
Caspian By the way, would you mind lighting a proper fire for us, Eustace.

The Dragon reacts

Edmund That was really tactless of you, Caspian.
Caspian Well, I merely thought ...
Drinian My Lord is right. We need rest and a good night's sleep. (*Aside*) Though only Aslan knows what we can do tomorrow to help the poor boy.

They lie down to sleep. The Dragon withdraws towards the cave. Reepicheep takes up a position on guard outside the cave. The Dragon can react to what follows. It is night. A bright full moon is shining

Caspian Drinian.
Drinian Sire?
Caspian Drinian, I've been thinking.
Drinian Sire.
Caspian The dragon might fit along one side of the deck.

Drinian We'd have to shift all the stores to the other side to balance the ship.

Caspian What about the sideways pull? Would it put too much strain on the *Dawn Treader*?

Drinian I'd have to think about that, Sire. And anyway, how do you feed a dragon?

Caspian Yes, that's a real problem. Good-night, Drinian.

Drinian Good-night, Sire.

Pause

Edmund Lucy, are you asleep?

Lucy Of course I'm not.

Edmund Perhaps we could tow him behind the ship.

Lucy Perhaps he could keep up by flying alongside us?

Edmund No, I don't think he could keep going for that long. And anyway, how do you feed a dragon?

Lucy Yes, that's a real problem.

Pause

Reepicheep Eustace, I am deeply sorry you have come to this sad pass. It is a striking illustration of the turn of fortune's wheel. In my humble home I have three books that tell of, oh, more than a hundred examples of emperors, kings, dukes, knights, all of whom fell from great prosperity into deep distress. Dear Dragon—I do beg your pardon—I mean, of course, dear Eustace—many of them recovered from their misfortune and lived happily ever afterwards. However, I have to say that your predicament is unusual in the extreme. You need help. And I fear that we, your companions, are unable to give you the right sort of help. Were I in your situation, I would think very hard about the utter, utter East, and the Great Lion, Aslan. He, I am sure, can break any enchantment, any spell. Well, I will leave you to sleep now, or do whatever it is that dragons do by night. If you should need me, just call. Well, just puff loudly . . . I'm a very light sleeper. Good-night, Eustace . . .

The Dragon withdraws into the cave

In the silence that follows, the silhouette of a dragon flies slowly across the face of the moon. We hear the roar of a lion and a series of terrible screams. All awake in panic

Drinian What in Aslan's name was that?

Lucy It was horrible—the most horrible sound I've ever heard.

Caspian We must arm and take up defensive positions. I will lead with King Edmund to my right, Captain Drinian to my left.

Reepicheep Sire, I protest.

Caspian I need you to guard our backs.

Reepicheep Guard your *backs*?

Caspian Just do as I say, will you!

They take up defensive positions. As Caspian instructs Reepicheep there is the sound of footsteps. Everyone prepares to do battle

Eustace enters

Eustace Are you there, Reep?
Reepicheep Is that really you, Eustace?
Eustace Yes, Reep, I'm back. Back as myself.
Reepicheep Welcome home, my friend.

All crowd around, welcoming him, with phrases like "Aslan be praised", "Safe back with us", "What a great relief"

Lucy Tell us what happened, Eustace.
Eustace Well, I was lying in the cave, in terrible pain, trying to sleep, thinking about what Reep had told me. Then I saw this huge lion coming towards me.
All Aslan!
Eustace I was terribly afraid—especially when it told me to follow it.
Reepicheep You mean the lion spoke to you?
Eustace No, I don't think he did. But he told me somehow, all the same. And I followed him a long way into the mountains to a sort of well of cool water. I knew that if I could only get into the water it would ease the pain in my leg. But the lion told me to get undressed first. So I tried to scratch myself, and first my dragon scales fell off, then my skin—just like peeling a banana. It was lovely, all the pain had gone. I was just going to step into the water, when I looked down and found the scales had all come back. I scratched off three sets of scales. Then the lion said—or told me somehow: "You will have to let *me* undress you". The first tear he made was so deep that I thought it had gone right into my heart. That's when I screamed. Well, he peeled it all off, picked me up, and threw me into the water. It stung like anything at first, but then all the pain went away and I had turned into a boy again. It was all like a bad dream. With a happy ending.
Reepicheep No, it wasn't a dream.
Eustace What do you think it was, then?
Reepicheep I think you've met Aslan.
Eustace I've heard that name so often. I was really beginning to hate it. Who is Aslan? Do you know him?
Reepicheep By the lion's mane, I hope to know him. He is the great Lion, the son of the emperor beyond the sea, who saved Narnia from the wicked White Witch. King Edmund and Queen Lucy have seen him. Prince Caspian too, I think. It may be Aslan's country we are sailing to, beyond the utter East.
Caspian Let's get back to the ship straightaway, I've seen enough of this place.

Eustace slides the armlet from his arm and gives it to Caspian

Edmund Well, we've discovered the fate of the Lord Octesian, at least.

Eustace He found the dragon's treasure like me, and in his turn became the guardian of the treasure. He turned into a dragon.

Caspian Treasure? What treasure?

Edmund The treasure in the cave, of course. Dragons always guard treasure.

Caspian You mean there's treasure here. And nobody told me? How much?

Eustace A very great deal. But . . .

Caspian Then we must take it on board. Drinian, get Rynelf and start loading . . .

Lucy Caspian? Have you taken leave of your senses?

Caspian What do you mean?

Edmund Everyone knows that dragon's treasure is cursed.

Drinian It's true, Prince Caspian.

Reepicheep I fear, Sire, that if we took that treasure back to Narnia, we would take the dragon's curse with us.

Caspian (*throwing the armlet away*) Then I suppose we must leave it. Leave all of it on this accursed Dragon's Island. For somebody else to find.

Drinian There will be other islands, Sire. And we still have five more Lords to find.

Reepicheep And the closer we get to the land of Aslan, the greater will be the rewards. Come, Sire.

Eustace All that glisters is not gold. That's what Ma and Pa say. And they're always right. Well, nearly always. I still haven't found a British Consul, you know.

Lucy I don't think you will, Eustace.

Edmund I wonder what *we* will find.

Rynelf enters running

Rynelf Captain! Prince Caspian! Captain! Captain!

Drinian What is it, Rynelf.

Rynelf I was up the mast repairing the sail. And I saw it.

Drinian Saw what, lad? Make a proper report!

Rynelf Just coming out of the haze—all strange and shimmery.

Caspian What, Rynelf? What did you see?

Rynelf A great big island. And it was covered in—well, it looked as though it was covered in gold!

Caspian You hear that? GOLD!

Caspian runs off

Lucy Caspian!

Edmund No, Caspian!

Eustace Reep!

Drinian I don't like the sound of this . . .

Reepicheep We must all put our trust in Aslan!

The roar of a lion

BLACK-OUT

ACT II

Scene 1

Deathwater Island

Lucy, Edmund, Eustace and Reepicheep enter

Lucy This new island is a beautiful place. It's just like Rynelf said, all strange and shimmery and hazy with gold.

Edmund It must be some trick of the sunlight. I suppose the farther east we go, the closer we get to the rising sun. So the combination of the morning sea mist and the early morning sun would tend to make everything shimmer. Like gold. It's all quite logical.

Eustace Well it's a big relief after Dragon Island, I can tell you. No smoke, no fire, and no caves.

Caspian, Drinian and Rynelf enter

Caspian It's not quite what I expected from Rynelf's report, Captain. Shimmery, yes. Hazy, yes. But it's not exactly covered in gold. Just earth and grass and stuff.

Rynelf It was just a figure of speech, Sire. A bit of poetic licence.

Drinian Address yourself to me, lad. (*To Caspian*) But there is one compensation, Sire. There's plenty of water for the ship's stores. Rynelf, get down to the *Dawn Treader*, check that she's all secure fore and aft, shipshape and Narnian fashion.

Rynelf I beg your pardon, Captain?

Drinian (*resigned*) Get down to the ship and check that she's——

Rynelf I heard the words you said, Captain, I just don't know what they mean.

Drinian Landlubber!

Caspian He meant go and see that the ship is safe and well, please, Rynelf.

Drinian And bring the water barrels back with you.

Rynelf Ay ay, Captain.

Rynelf exits

Caspian As for me, I'm going to sit down by this pool of lovely, cool, ice-blue water and have a long refreshing drink . . .

Eustace Me too.

Reepicheep }
Lucy   (*together*) LOOK!

Edmund What?

Lucy In the water. At the bottom of the pool.

Edmund Why, it's the golden statue of a man.

Lucy It's beautiful. Absolutely beautiful.

Caspian Well, that was worth coming to see. Gold, eh? I wonder if we can get it out.

Lucy How deep is the water?

Caspian No way of telling.

Edmund Try using my sword.

Drinian takes the sword and lowers it into the pool

Lucy It's not gold at all. It's the sunlight. Look, your sword's turned the same colour.

Drinian lets go of the sword

Edmund What's wrong?

Drinian I couldn't hold it. It suddenly seemed so heavy.

Reepicheep And there it is on the bottom—and Queen Lucy is right, the sword is the same colour as the statue.

Edmund Get back! Back from the water. At once. All of you. It's real danger!

They all do

Look, look at the toes of my boots.

Eustace They look a bit yellow.

Edmund They're gold. Solid gold. Feel them. They're as heavy as lead.

Caspian By Aslan! You don't mean to say . . .

Edmund Yes I do! The water turns things to gold. My sword, the toes of my boots . . .

Lucy And that isn't a gold statue at all . . . It's the body of a man.

Edmund And look, he's wearing a Narnian armlet.

Caspian Lord Restimar!

Edmund He must have been hot, thirsty, gone for a swim, and . . .

Lucy How horrible.

Edmund What a narrow escape for all of us, though.

Reepicheep Narrow indeed. Anyone's finger, foot, whisker, or tail might have slipped into the water at any moment.

Caspian (*thoughtfully*) The king who owned this island would soon be the richest of all the kings in the world.

Drinian Then you must claim it, Sire.

Caspian I claim this land on behalf of the King of Narnia. And I bind you all to secrecy. No-one must know of the island. On pain of death, do you all hear me!

Edmund Who do you think you're talking to, Caspian? I am not your subject. I am one of the four ancient Kings of Narnia and you are under allegiance to me. If anyone claims the island, it should be me.

Caspian So it has come to that has it, King Edmund. (*He goes to attack Edmund*)

Lucy Stop it, both of you. You can't quarrel over gold. It's stupid. Oh if only Aslan were here, he'd stop you fighting . . . ooh! (*She points*)

Everyone except Reepicheep turns

Aslan appears, dazzling bright. He roars and disappears

Reepicheep My Lords, this is a place with a curse on it. Let us go back to the ship at once. And may I suggest that we rename this island "Deathwater Island".

All turn back rubbing their eyes

Caspian What were we talking about? I feel I've been making a fool of myself. "Deathwater Island" certainly sounds like a suitable name, Reep, though I for the life of me can't think why.

Drinian Something tells me we ought to be off, Sire.

Lucy Have we been asleep? I dreamt such a silly dream.

Edmund I can't remember. I suppose we must have, mustn't we. I had a silly dream, too. I dreamt that we were all——

Eustace Here's Rynelf.

Rynelf enters

Drinian I thought I told you to bring the water barrels, Rynelf.

Rynelf The strangest thing has happened, Captain. When I got back to the ship, the barrels were already full. To the brim. With clear, cold, fresh water.

Reepicheep Did it taste sweet?

Rynelf Well, no, Sir Mouse. It tasted just like water, really.

Caspian Three Lords found, four to go. I hope we find the rest alive . . .

Eustace We seem no nearer to your heart's desire, Reep.

Reepicheep Our progress may seem slow, my friend—but we keep moving on to the East, the utter East. And the adventures grow more and more unusual—that you must admit!

Caspian Come on everyone, back to the *Dawn Treader*. I wonder what we'll discover next.

All exit except Reepicheep and Caspian

Reepicheep And I wonder what adventures Aslan has in store for us on the next island.

They exit

SCENE 2

The Island of Silence

All enter, except Lucy, laughing and chattering about the new island and how bare and plain everything is. They exit

Lucy enters

Lucy Wait for me. Oh, please, wait for me. Caspian, I thought you said we should never split up on a strange island . . . Oh, curses, I've got a stone in my shoe. (*She sits down on the ground*)

A gentle thumping is heard in the distance

Those boys have no thought whatsoever for anything but adventure.

The thumping is getting louder

And Reep's just as bad, and getting worse. The further east we get, the more thoughtful he gets. What's that thumping noise?

The thumping is getting near very quickly

That's peculiar. It could be dangerous. I'd better hide.

As Lucy hides, the thumping noise gets louder and louder and suddenly stops

Lucy starts to come out of hiding, but retreats rapidly as the following dialogue between the Thumpers is heard

Chief's voice Mates, now's our chance!
Thumper 1's voice That's it, now's our chance!
Thumper 2's voice He's right. He's right. The Chief's right again.
Thumper 3's voice You never said a truer word. He's never wrong, mates.
Chief's voice What I say is, we must get down to the shore between those strangers and their boat. Then we can catch them all when they try to put to sea.
Thumper 1's voice That's it, catch them all when they try to put to sea.
Thumper 2's voice He's right again. The Chief's always right.
Thumper 3's voice And he's never wrong. No, never.
Thumper 4's voice You never made a better plan, Chief. Never made a better plan.
Thumper 2's voice He's right, you know. He's right.
Thumper 3's voice Who is?
Thumper 2's voice Why he is.
Thumper 3's voice Who?
Thumper 2's voice Why, he.
Chief's voice Lively now, lads, lively. Look to your weapons. Off we go.
Thumper 4's voice Right again, Chief. You never gave a better order. Just what we were going to say ourselves. Off we go.

The Thumpers set off, with Thumpers 2 and 3 still trying to sort out

Thumper 3's voice But who is?
Thumper 2's voice Why he is, of course.
Thumper 3's voice But who is he?
Thumper 2's voice He is.

The thumping dies off in the distance

Lucy comes out of hiding

Lucy That's terrible. I must tell the others at once. Oh, thank goodness, they're here.

All enter

What a relief, you're here. We're in terrible danger.

Edmund What do you mean, Lucy.

Lucy Terrible, terrible danger. Some people have just rushed past me, and are planning to catch us all when we go back to the boat.

Reepicheep Were there many?

Lucy It sounded like dozens to me. And that's not the worst of it.

Edmund Go on then, Lucy.

Lucy Well, you'll find it hard to believe, but they're invisible.

All start to laugh, except Drinian

Drinian That's not hard to believe at all, my Lords. We've seen some pretty strange things here already.

They stop laughing

Edmund This could be very serious indeed. Have you any idea what kind of people they were, Lucy?

Lucy How could I when I couldn't see them? But they didn't seem to have any feet, only voices and this thumping noise, like a mallet hitting the ground.

Reepicheep I wonder, do they become visible when you drive a sword into them?

Drinian We may well find out, soon enough. And we'd better get away from here. For all we know, there could be one standing right beside us listening to every word we say.

Caspian Let's go down to the boat and try to negotiate with them. (*Hastily*) Just as a first step, Reep——

Chief's voice Don't move no further, masters, no further now. There's fifty and more of us here with weapons in our fists.

Thumper 2's voice He's right. He's right. Fifty or more. Probably as many as forty-five.

Thumper 3's voice Fifty-five, he means. He's never wrong, our Chief.

Thumper 1's voice You can depend on what he says. He's telling you the truth.

Reepicheep I do not see these fifty warriors . . .

Chief's voice That's right. That's right. That's because we're invisible.

Thumper 4's voice Keep it up, Chief. Keep it up. You couldn't ask for a better answer than that.

Caspian Invisible people, what do you want with us? I am Caspian, King of Narnia, and I demand to know what you want with us.

Chief's voice We don't want *you*.

Thumpers' voices No more we do. No more we do.

Chief's voice We want the little girl. There is a job she had to do for us. On her own.

Reepicheep The little girl, you dogs, is a queen.

Chief's voice We don't know about dogs, or queens or kings of Narnia.

Thumpers' voices No more we do. No more we do.

Chief's voice But there is a job that the little girl simply has to do for us. Of her own free will. On her own.

Lucy What is it?

Reepicheep If it is against Her Majesty's honour, you will be amazed to see how many of you will die.

Chief's voice Well, it's like this. This island is the property of a great, great magician and we are all his servants. One day, this magician fell into a great rage. And he put a spell on us. An uglifying spell. He made us all so ugly we couldn't bear to look at each other.

Thumpers' voices No indeed, no, no.

Chief's voice So one afternoon we crept upstairs as bold as brass to see what we could do. We found his great book of spells and did a magic. But we made ourselves invisible. Well, not we exactly. It has to be a little girl as does the magic of her own free will and on her own. My little girl, Clipsie, she did it for us, so we needn't see how uglified we were any more. But she did it so well that she invisibled the great magician, too. And now we don't know where he is, or whether he's dead or alive or coming or going and it's getting on our nerves. And that's our sad, sad story.

The Thumpers weep with sadness

Lucy But what has all this got to do with us?

Chief's voice Have I gone and left out the whole point?

Thumpers' voice No, Chief. Not you.

Chief's voice My little girl's too old to do the magic, now. So we've been waiting for a nice little girl from foreign parts like you, Miss, to remove the spell for us and make us visible again.

Thumper 1's voice That's right, Chief, a nice little girl like her.

Edmund But haven't you any other little girls of your own?

Thumper 4's voice Course we have. Course we've little girls of our own.

Eustace Well, why don't you ask one of them to do the magic?

Thumpers' voices He's right. He's right. Why don't we ask one of them to do it, Chief?

Chief's voice Because we dursn't.

Thumpers' voices That's right. Because we dursn't.

Reepicheep Dursn't? Dursn't? This is a word completely new to me. Pray, can anyone explain it?

Lucy They dare not, Reepicheep. They are afraid.

Caspian Well, that's outrageous. To ask a lady to face dangers alone that you daren't face yourself is, is, well, it's . . .

Reepicheep Dishonourable is the word you are looking for, Sire.

Lucy I'll do it.

Others What? Don't be silly!

Lucy Don't try to stop me. There are obviously dozens of them. They say they're heavily armed.

Reepicheep I beg leave to doubt that, my lady.

A spear appears, quivering at his feet

Chief's voice That's a spear that is. They come visible when they leave our hands.

Lucy As I was saying, they are obviously heavily armed. We can't fight them, because we can't see them. I don't want to be cut to bits by invisible spears and swords and things. So let's try the other way, and help them.

Caspian What would you do, Reep?

Reepicheep Her Majesty is right. The service they ask of her is a noble and heroic deed. If her heart moves her to risk the magician, I will not speak against it, but support her with all my might and main.

Caspian And so I.

Drinian And I.

Eustace And I.

Edmund And I.

Chief's voice Three cheers for the little girl!

Thumpers' voices Hip hip hurray. Hip hip hurray. Hip hip hurray. Hip hip hurray.

They all exit, except Lucy

The upstairs of the house comes into view. It consists of a room lined with books. The focal point is a huge book lying on a huge lectern. Lucy begins to turn the pages; her voice echoes slightly

Lucy What a beautiful book. Without doubt the most beautiful book I have ever seen. What have we here? Spells, of course. Here's a cure for warts. Wash in a silver basin by moonlight ... Well, I haven't got any warts, so that's no good. Here's one for toothache, and one for cramp, and another for lifting a swarm of bees. Fascinating. This one's for finding buried treasure, and here's another for remembering forgotten things—that could be really useful. Here's how to raise a wind, or fog, or rain, snow, hail or ice. My word, that's a very beautiful page. What does it say? "A spell to make her that utters it beautiful beyond the lot of mortals." Just think of that. To be the most beautiful woman on earth. Why princes and kings would come to ask for my hand in marriage; they would fight tournaments and mock battles for my favours; then perhaps the battles would become real ones and nation would fight nation for the honour of having me as queen and then Narnia would be laid waste together with all the lands around it. But that wouldn't matter, as long as every woman was jealous of my beauty and my power, and every man worshipped me but hopelessly, and oh! I will say that spell. I must say that spell.

The page of the book becomes a picture of Aslan. The picture roars in anger. Lucy is very frightened and turns over the page quickly

That was silly of me. I nearly got carried away. What's this next one? A spell that lets you know what your friends really say about you. That could be interesting. I'll say it quickly. (*She mumbles to herself*)

The sound of a railway train

How strange. That's a train. And that's a compartment, and there are my two schoolfriends, Marjorie Preston and Anne Featherstone.

The page of the book becomes a picture of two girls sitting in a railway compartment

Anne's voice Will we be friends this term? Or are you still soft on that Lucy Pevensie girl?

Marjorie's voice Don't know what you mean by "soft on".

Anne's voice Oh yes, you do. You were always with her last term.

Marjorie's voice No, I wasn't. I've got more sense than that. She's not a bad little kid in her way. But very secretive and a bit boring. I was getting pretty tired of her by the end of term.

Lucy (*shouting*) Well, you won't get the chance to be bored next term, Marjorie Preston, you two-faced beast.

The picture fades, and Lucy turns the page

Well, I thought she was a lot nicer than that, I wonder if all my friends are the same. I don't want to know, really. What's this next one. "A spell for the refreshment of the spirit." That sounds nice. (*She starts to read. Silence as she reads through three pages. A sigh. Pause*) That was the loveliest story I've ever read or shall ever read in my life. I think I'll read it all over again. (*She tries to turn back the pages*) Oh, what a shame, I can't turn back. The pages are stuck or something. Now, what's this? A page with no pictures. Just some writing. What does it say? "A spell to make hidden things visible." That's it! That's the one I've been looking for. (*She chants the spell*) Is it working? Yes, it is: there are pictures on the page now.

The sound of the soft, heavy pad of footfalls is heard

I wonder if the Thumpers are visible now. I wonder what else I've made visible. What's that noise: is it the magician? Will he be really angry with me?

Aslan appears

Aslan! The highest of all high kings! Dearest, dearest Aslan! How wonderful to see you again ... When did you arrive?

Aslan (*purring*) I have been here all the time. You have made me visible.

Lucy How could you say such a thing, Aslan. As if anything *I* did could make *you* visible.

Aslan But you did, Lucy. Do you think I wouldn't obey my own rules? And speaking of rules, you've been eavesdropping, Lucy. On your school-friends.

Lucy Yes, I have. And I'll never speak to Marjorie Preston again. But I thought because it was magic ...

Aslan Spying on people by magic is the same as spying on them in any other way. You have misjudged your friend. She is weak, but she likes you. She was simply saying what she thought the other girl wanted to hear.

Lucy I don't think I'll ever be able to forget what I heard her say.

Aslan No, you won't.

Lucy Oh, Aslan. Have I spoiled everything? If it hadn't been for this, would we have gone on being friends? Would we have been really great friends all our lives? And now never shall?

Aslan Child, no-one is ever told what *would* have happened.

Lucy Then shall I never be able to read that story again? The one where the pages got stuck? What was it called—"a spell for the refreshment of the spirit"? That was the loveliest story I've ever read . . . Will you tell it to me, Aslan?

Aslan Indeed I will, Lucy. For years and years and years to come. But now we must meet the master of this house. Come, Coriakin, come!

Coriakin, the magician, enters

Coriakin Welcome, my Lord, to the least of your houses.

Aslan Coriakin, these foolish creatures I have given you to rule—are you weary of them?

Coriakin No, Sire, not at all. They are stupid, but there is no real harm in them. Indeed, I have grown very fond of them. Sometimes I am a little impatient with them, wishing wisdom would come to them more quickly than it can.

Aslan All in good time, Coriakin. All in good time.

Coriakin I know, I know. Would you care to see them, Sire?

Aslan Nay, I fear I would frighten them out of what little sense they have. Many stars will grow old and come to their rest in these islands before your people become ready to meet me. And I must be off to Cair Paravel, to encourage Trumpkin the Dwarf who is counting the days till Caspian comes home. Do not look so sad, Lucy. We shall meet again, soon.

Lucy But Aslan, what do you call *soon*?

Aslan I call all times "soon".

Aslan vanishes

Coriakin Gone! And both you and I are quite crestfallen, young lady. It's always like that. But you can't keep him, you know. He's wild. Not like a tame lion. And how did you enjoy my book of spells?

Lucy Parts of it were very good indeed. Other parts were a bit scary. Did you know I was there all the time?

Coriakin I was rather sleepy today. Not on guard at all. Though I knew that when the Duffers magicked themselves——

Lucy Pardon me for interrupting, but what did you call them?

Coriakin Duffers. It's short for Dufflepud, you see.

Lucy doesn't, but is too polite to interrupt

When the Duffers magicked themselves, I knew, of course, that you or someone like you would come along to remove the spell, but I wasn't quite sure of when.

Lucy When will my magic work?

Coriakin It has worked, already. They're visible right now.

Lucy Why *did* you uglify them?

Coriakin Well, because they wouldn't do what they were told. The troubles I've had with them. One day I found them planting boiled potatoes. They said it was so that when the potatoes grew they'd be all ready to eat. Some of them are here now.

The Thumpers, now visible, enter

Thumper 1 Hey, lads, we're visible.

Chief Visible, we are, lads. And what I say is, when lads are visible, why, they can see one another.

Thumper 2 He's right. He's right. The Chief's right yet again, lads.

Thumper 3 He's never wrong.

Thumper 4 Straight to the point, as always. No-one's got a clearer head than you, Chief.

Lucy They're not ugly at all. They're really quite sweet. I don't think you should change them back. They're so funny and really very nice. Would it help if I told them that?

Coriakin I think it would help a great deal. If you could ever get it into their silly heads.

Chief Well, lads, we are mortal ugly, and that's a fact.

Thumper 2 That's right. He's right.

Thumper 1 You've said it all, Chief. We are mortal ugly.

Lucy But I don't think you are ugly at all. I think you look very nice.

Thumper 2 She's right, she's right.

Thumper 3 She's never wrong, mates.

Thumper 4 True, Missie. You could never find a handsomer lot.

Thumper 1 Handsome's the word. We're right handsome.

Chief She's a saying as how we looked very nice before we was uglified.

Lucy I'm not saying that at all. I said you're very nice *now*.

Chief That's what I said you said. That we would be very nice if we weren't what we looked like now.

Lucy But ...

Coriakin Lucy, they'll never change ...

Lucy (*sadly*) No, they'll never change.

Thumper 4 So it's back to work, is it, Chief?

Chief It's back to work, lads.

Thumper 4 You never gave a better order, Chief.

Thumper 2 He's right, you know.

As all Thumpers exit, Thumpers 2 and 3 are still trying to sort out

Thumper 3 Who is?

Thumper 2 Why he is.

Thumper 3 Who?

Thumper 2 Why he.
Thumper 3 But who is *he*?
Coriakin And you must go too, Lucy, back to the ship, back to all your
friends. I will conjure up a favourable wind for you so you may follow the
four noble Lords to the utter, utter East. Farewell, Queen Lucy.
Lucy Farewell, Coriakin, farewell.

Lucy exits

Coriakin And may your journey be more fortunate than that of the four
great Lords—for they sailed away seven years to this day and have never
been seen again since. Come, you sisters of the wind, come and give me a
goodly, gentle breeze. Send these travellers and their ship, the valiant
Dawn Treader, on and on safely into the utter, utter East.

> A north wind will bring chill
> An east wind will bring ill
> A south wind slow their trip
> A west wind speed their ship
> into the utter East.

Come sisters, give me a good west wind!

The wind rises

Black-out

SCENE 3

The Dawn Treader *at sea*

Lucy And then the magician Coriakin said that the four noble Lords had
visited his island and sailed on into the utter, utter East.
Reepicheep So at least we know they got this far.
Drinian And had stores and courage enough to be able to go on.
Rynelf Land ho! Island, ahead. Two points to the port beam. At least, I
think it is.
Drinian Rynelf. I've warned you before about being precise. Is it or isn't it?
Lucy Remember, he's been right before, Captain. It's getting very cold, isn't
it?
Rynelf Well, whatever it is is certainly two points off the port beam. And it's
less of an island, and more of a darkness. If you know what I mean. Like a
tunnel. No, like a black mist. No, well ...
Drinian Rynelf, you're impossible. Will you make a proper report, man!
Rynelf Well, come forrard and see for yourself, Captain. It's coming up
fast.

Drinian hands over the helm and starts towards the prow

Drinian Prince Caspian, we are heading towards a black mist.

Caspian Do we go into this?

Drinian Not by my advice, Sire.

Edmund I don't think we have much choice.

Reepicheep And why not, Sire? Here is as great an adventure as ever I heard of.

Eustace Your sense of adventure will get us into terrible trouble, Reep.

The stage darkens

Lucy It's getting very, very dark.

Reepicheep Fear not, Queen Lucy. I am here to watch over you.

Lucy Then, on we go.

Caspian Battle stations, everyone.

The darkness is total. There is complete silence for a moment. Then an inhuman scream of terror. Reactions of: "What in all Narnia was that?", "In Aslan's name" etc.

Reepicheep Who calls to us? If you are foe, we do not fear you. If you are friend, your enemies shall suffer for the hurt they have caused you.

Rhoop *(calling)* Mercy! mercy! I am Lord Rhoop of Narnia.

All Lord Rhoop?

Caspian The fourth of my missing Lords.

Rhoop I was washed overboard and lost at sea an age ago. Even if you are only one more dream, take me on board. Take me on board, and strike me dead, if you will. But in the name of Aslan, do not leave me in this horrible place.

Caspian Where are you? Where are you? Come aboard and welcome!

Edmund I see him, Caspian. Eustace, help me!

Drinian Stand by to bring him aboard. Rynelf, we'll need a berth, warm blankets and hot drink.

Rhoop is hauled on board

Rhoop Fly! Fly! Turn your ship away from here. Fly away from this accursed shore.

Reepicheep Calm yourself, man. Tell us what the danger is. We are not used to running away.

Rhoop Well, you had best learn how. This is the Island Where Dreams Come True.

Rynelf The Island Where Dreams Come True, eh? I've been searching for that island for a long time. I reckon I'd be married to my sweetheart, if I were there.

Drinian And I'd find my brother alive again.

Lucy And I'd be with Aslan again.

Edmund And I'd be hunting with Caspian in the forest lands of Narnia.

Eustace And I'd be safe home again together with Ma and Pa.

Caspian And I would have found my missing Lords and met my own true queen.

Reepicheep And I'd find the utter, utter East.

Rhoop Fools! That's exactly the way I thought. But this is the island where dreams, not day-dreams, but real dreams of the blackest night come true.

Edmund You mean—you mean, nightmares? A land where nightmares come true?

A moment's silence. Then, total panic

Caspian Starboard the helm, Captain. Sail for all our lives.

Reepicheep This is a panic, Sire. This is a rout.

Caspian Dreams of the night that are real, Reep. There are some things no man can face.

Reepicheep Then it is my good fortune not to be a man!

Edmund That sounds like a huge pair of scissors opening and shutting over there . . .

Caspian Hush, I can hear things crawling all over the ship.

Drinian I can hear it too. A great slug sliding down the mast.

Rynelf Gongs, I knew there'd be huge gongs ringing.

Eustace I'm falling and falling and falling into the black, black well.

Lucy Spiders. Creepy, crawly spiders. There are spiders running everywhere. All over you. All over me.

Rynelf We'll never get out, the Captain's steering us in circles! We're going round and round and round and round.

Drinian It's the wave. I can see it. The great wave at the edge of the world! We'll all be sucked over the edge. Turn away, turn away.

Reepicheep Don't turn away. Sail east, not west. Sail east, Captain Drinian, or we'll never get out.

Rhoop Never get out! That's it! We'll never get out! What a fool I am . . . No, we'll never ever get out. We'll fall over the edge of the world.

Lucy Aslan, Aslan, if you ever loved us, send us help now!

All ASLAN! ASLAN!

Rynelf Light! Light ahead.

A searchlight beam hits the Dawn Treader

Caspian Drinian, follow the light! Surely Aslan has sent us a guide to lead us out of darkness.

Reepicheep Lead on, dear light. Lead us ever eastwards.

Caspian Guide us out of the darkness to the last three noble Lords.

The darkness begins to lighten into a most glorious blue

SCENE 4

The Island of the Sleepers

We see tall pillars, an open space and a table set for a banquet. At it sit three haystacks, the Lords Revilian, Argoz and Mavramorn, snoring. There is a door UL

Caspian, Reepicheep, Lucy, Edmund and Eustace enter

Caspian Are they real? Are they dead?

Reepicheep I think not, Sire. All three are snoring fast asleep.

Edmund It must have been a long sleep to let their hair grow like this.

Lucy An enchanted sleep. I knew the moment we landed that this island was full of magic.

Eustace But can we break the enchantment?

Caspian We can try. (*He shakes Revilian*)

Edmund Did he speak? What did he say?

Caspian He said: "I'll travel eastward no more. Up sail for Narnia" . . . He's even more asleep now.

Drinian shakes Argoz

Reepicheep This one said, "On, on to the East—the utter East. To the land behind the sun!"

Caspian shakes Mavramorn

Caspian And this one? Did I hear right?

Lucy Yes. He said "Could you pass the mustard, please".

Eustace Do you think the food could be drugged?

Edmund Up sail for Narnia, eh? They must be Narnians.

Caspian Check their rings and their devices, Drinian. I think we have found the rest of my missing Lords.

Reepicheep Aslan be praised, they are safe. And alive.

Caspian And asleep. Our quest is at its end.

Lucy Thanks be to Aslan.

All Thanks be to Aslan!

The door UL *opens, a figure carrying a candlestick is silhouetted against the doorway, the door shuts. Ramandu's Daughter enters*

Daughter Travellers. You have come so far to reach Aslan's table. Why do you not eat and drink?

Caspian Most beautiful lady, we feared the food was drugged and had cast our friends into enchanted sleep.

Daughter They have never tasted it.

Lucy Please, what happened to them?

Daughter Seven years ago they came here in a ship whose sail was rags and whose timbers were full of leaks. When they reached this table, they quarrelled and one lay his hand upon the Knife of Stone and would have fought with his friends. But it is not a right thing for him to touch, and so deep sleep fell upon all three of them.

Eustace What is this Knife of Stone?

Lucy I have seen it before, I think. The White Witch used a knife like this when she killed Aslan at the Stone Table.

Daughter It is the same. It was brought here to be kept in honour as long as the world shall last.

Edmund I'm not a coward, I think. And I don't mean to be rude. But a lot of strange things have happened to us on this voyage. Things aren't always what they seem. How do we know that you are a friend? How do we know that you aren't a witch?

Daughter You cannot know. You can only believe.

Reepicheep Sire, of your courtesy, fill me a cup with wine from that flagon. It is too big for me to lift. I would drink a toast to this most beauteous lady.

Caspian pours him a cup

Reepicheep Lady, I pledge you. (*He drinks*)

Everyone watches him. Nothing happens. They fall to

Lucy Why is it called Aslan's table?

Daughter It was set here by his bidding for those who travel so far. Some call this island the World's End, for though you can sail further, this is the beginning of the end.

Eustace How does the food keep fresh?

Daughter It is eaten and renewed every day.

Caspian And how, fairest of ladies, do we wake the sleepers to take them home? Queen Lucy once told me of a story where a king or a prince, I think, dissolved a magic enchantment by kissing a sleeping princess.

Daughter Here, the Prince cannot kiss the Princess until after he has dissolved the magic.

Caspian Then in the name of Aslan, sweet maiden show me how to dissolve the magic.

Daughter My father, Ramandu, will teach you that.

All Your father?

Lucy Who is he?

The door opens and Ramandu enters

Daughter Look! (*She points to the doorway*)

Dawn is breaking

Ramandu and his Daughter turn to the dawn and incant a high beautiful sound that is a song to the early morning. Sunrise takes place. With it comes the sound of thousands of birds. As Ramandu and his Daughter turn back, we see that the table has been cleared

Lucy Look! Look! The table has been cleared!

Edmund So *that's* how it's done! At dawn, the birds clear it all away.

Daughter And at dusk the birds lay the table again!

Ramandu With the freshest and choicest of foods from all over the world.

Caspian Sir, will you tell us how to break the enchantment that keeps these three Lords asleep?

Ramandu Gladly, my son. To break the enchantment, you must sail to the East, to the World's End, and then come back to this island having left at least one of your number behind.

Reepicheep And what is to happen to the one that is left behind, honoured Sir?

Ramandu He must journey on to the utter East and never return into this world.

Reepicheep That of course is my heart's only desire.

Caspian And are we near the World's End now, Sir?

Ramandu I have no sailor's knowledge, and cannot help you in this. I have heard of a great white sea that lies at the end of the world. But who knows—since no-one has ever been there and come back. But I must know what is your resolve. Will you sail East into the unknown and then leave one of your number behind? Or do you prefer to turn westward and sail home?

Caspian Well, my friends?

Reepicheep There can be no question, Sire. It is plainly part of our quest to rescue these three Lords from enchantment.

Eustace They wouldn't be much use fast asleep for ever back at home.

Caspian It *is* part of our quest. But what we should say to Drinian and Rynelf. They volunteered to find seven Lords, not to sail to the edge of the world, to the utter East.

Rhoop, Rynelf and Drinian enter

Ramandu It would be no use your sailing to the World's End with men unwilling or deceived.

Caspian Drinian, I ordered you back to the ship.

Drinian Pardon me, Sire, the Lord Rhoop asked to see his old shipmates.

Rhoop Prince Caspian, I ordered the Captain to bring me here.

Caspian (*to Ramandu*) Sir, this Narnian Lord has suffered greatly. He has been on the Island of Dreams for seven years.

Ramandu Then this man needs sleep without measure. I can give him what his friends already enjoy, sleep without any form of dream, without any interruption, until you return.

Rhoop I accept, gladly.

Caspian Drinian, Rynelf, we have a choice to make. We have found the last of the seven Lords—our quest is over. But these Lords will sleep for ever unless we travel on to the edge of the world. Will you continue the journey with us?

Rynelf All the winds since we left have been westerly. How can we sail all the way back against the wind? How will we ever see Narnia again?

Drinian That's landsman's talk, Rynelf.

Rynelf Why can't we stay here for the winter and voyage home in the spring?

Eustace What would you do for supplies?

Ramandu This table will be filled with a king's feast every day at sunset.

Rynelf Now you're talking! I vote we stay here.

Drinian Hold hard, lad. There's something I'd like to say. Not one of us was pressed to make this journey. We're all volunteers. Apart from our three friends there. And there's one here who would stay and enjoy a king's feast every day who was talking very loud about adventure and glory on the day we sailed from Narnia. And I recollect one who swore he wouldn't come home till he'd found the very end of the world. And if I remember correctly, we had to fight people off who wanted to come with us — because it was reckoned nobler to be a sailor aboard the *Dawn Treader* than to win a knight's spurs. What I'm trying to say to you, Rynelf, is that if we come home and say we'd got to the beginning of the World's End, but hadn't the heart to go further, we'll look as silly as those there Dufflepuds.

Rynelf For once, Captain, you're absolutely right. I vote we go on.

Caspian So now, my friends and companions of the great ship the *Dawn Treader* let us make our farewells to Ramandu and his most beautiful daughter. Lady, I hope to speak with you again. And with your father, when I have broken the enchantments. And so friends, let us sail on to the East, to the very end of the world.

Daughter Farewell, Caspian. Hurry back and speak with me again.

Caspian Fair lady, I promise on my oath as king so to do.

Ramandu Go with all good speed, brave travellers. May Aslan be with you, then, sooner than you think, you will reach your journey's end. Come daughter.

All exit

SCENE 5

The Dawn Treader *at sea*

The sail hangs dead, but the ship is moving. Caspian, Lucy, Edmund, Eustace, Reepicheep, Drinian and Rynelf are on deck

Lucy (*looking at the sea*) How beautifully clear the water is. You can see the shadow of the ship running along the bottom of the sea. What's that waving in the water? It's like trees waving in a wind.

Edmund Like a submarine forest.

Eustace And those pale streaks look like roads in the middle of a forest. What are those spiky bits?

Edmund They look like towers, and spires.

Lucy Like a town or a huge castle.

Reepicheep has hauled a bucket aboard and is drinking from it

Lucy I think I can see little people.

Eustace Yes, there. And there. Riding on horses.

Edmund Sea-horses. They're carrying spears.

Lucy They're hunting. They must be hunting fish.

Reepicheep Sweet. Sweet, sweet.

Drinian He's delirious. It's because he's seen mermen and mermaids. It sometimes gets them like that!

Reepicheep Where the waves grow sweet, there is the utter East. Sweet! Sweet!

Caspian (*laughing*) Reepicheep! It is sweet. It's wonderful. I'm not sure that it isn't going to kill me, but if so it is the death I would have chosen for myself. It's like—like drinking light.

Reepicheep That's what it's like. Drinkable light. We must be very near the end of the world now.

Lucy (*drinking*) It's the loveliest thing I've ever tasted. But it's so strong and filling. We won't need to eat anything now.

Drinian It's very strange, but there's not a breath of wind—the sail hangs dead. And yet we drive on as fast as if there was a gale behind us.

Caspian We must be in a very strong current.

Edmund It could be the wave at the edge of the world.

Caspian You mean, we might get poured over it, like a waterfall?

Reepicheep Yes, yes. That's just how I imagined it. The world as a great round table and the waters of the oceans pouring over the edge of it.

Rynelf Whiteness ahead. Whiteness dead ahead.

Drinian Not again. Rynelf, will you try and give proper calls?

Rynelf It is whiteness, Captain. As far as my eyes can see.

Caspian We'd better try and anchor, Captain. It might be dangerous.

Drinian Drop anchor, Rynelf.

Rynelf Lilies. A sea of lilies.

Drinian (*incredulous*) Sire, Rynelf reports we're approaching a sea of lilies.

Caspian Ramandu said a great white sea lay at the World's End. We must be at the end of the world.

Rynelf Water's shallowing very quickly, Cap'n.

Caspian We'd better anchor, Drinian. Friends, we have now fulfilled our quest. The seven Lords that my wicked Uncle Miraz sent away never to be found again are all accounted for. Thankfully, some are still alive. We, my friends, have reached the edge of the world and can go no further. Sir Reepicheep has sworn never to return—all of which means the three sleeping Lords are free of enchantment. To you, my beloved Lord Captain Drinian, I entrust the *Dawn Treader*. I command you to sail back to Narnia with all the speed you may. And if I come not again, it is my will that——

Drinian Come not again, Sire?

Lucy I knew he was up to something.

Caspian I have decided I am going on together with Reepicheep.

Edmund Caspian, you can't do this.

Reepicheep Most certainly, his Majesty cannot.

Drinian No, indeed. It's desertion.

Caspian Cannot? Desertion? How dare you question me?

Rynelf Begging your Majesty's pardon, but if one of us did the same, *you'd* call it desertion.

Drinian He's perfectly right.

Caspian By the mane of Aslan, I had thought you were all my subjects here. I will be obeyed.

Edmund I am not your subject. And I say you cannot do this.

Caspian I can! I can do anything! I am the King!

Reepicheep Indeed you are! You are the King of all Narnia. If you do not return, you break faith with all your people. You cannot go on adventures as if you were a private person. And if you will not listen, then everyone of us on board will join me in disarming and binding you till you come to your senses.

Edmund Quite right. Like they did with Ulysses.

Caspian And you're all against me? Even you, Lucy?

Lucy Remember you made a king's promise to Ramandu's daughter . . .

Caspian (*hesitating*) My own true queen. Well, yes. There is that. But I have changed my royal mind. That is my right, as king, is it not? I have decided to go on. I will not be overruled.

Edmund Caspian, what you propose is thoroughly dishonourable. Completely, unutterably, shameful. You cannot be serious. You, Caspian, have made promises that you have to keep. If you go on with Reep, you break faith with Ramandu's daughter. And with that gentle man, Ramandu. You break faith with the Lords who died. And with the three—no, the *four*—enchanted Lords left on Ramandu's island. You break faith with us, your companions, and with your people, the people of Narnia. You would break faith with Aslan himself. Who are you then—faithless—you are no better than your Uncle Miraz . . .

Caspian You presume too much, King Edmund! How dare you! I am determined. I am going below to make ready . . .

Caspian goes below deck

Edmund Drinian, Rynelf, all of you. Listen! This is madness. He cannot go on with Reep. When he comes on deck, we are going to have to tie him down, bind him and gag him. He has made promises. He has a country to rule. He has sworn oaths. He has a huge responsibility. A duty. He cannot toss it aside.

Lucy Oh, Aslan, we need your help more now than ever before. Please Aslan, help Caspian to come to his senses.

Pause. The roar of a lion

Edmund Eustace, Lucy, get ready—say your farewells. Reep, please stay with us as long as you feel it is right.

As they busy themselves preparing to leave:

Caspian enters

Caspian It's no good. For all my bad temper and showing off, it was no good. Aslan has spoken to me. He said—oh, well he said, and he was quite a bit stern with me—and he told me that all three of you are to go on with Reep, and I'm to go back. With Drinian and Rynelf. And at once. And what *is* the good of anything?

Lucy Caspian, dear, you knew we would have to go back.

Caspian But not when. And now's too soon.

Edmund You'll feel better when you get to Ramandu's island.

Caspian Captain, cast off! Friends, go quickly, my heart is breaking with sadness.

The Dawn Treader *sails away with Caspian, Drinian and Rynelf on board*

A silence. The Children and Reepicheep have formed themselves into a tight boatlike group, with Edmund at the prow

Lucy Look, look at the rainbow!

Edmund (*standing up and shading his eyes*) There it is . . .

Eustace What?

Edmund The great wave that is the end of the world! And beyond it, beyond even the sun . . .

Reepicheep Yes?

Edmund Mountains. Hanging up high into the sky. Warm and green and full of forests and waterfalls. Just listen to that sound.

Eustace It's enough to break your heart with happiness.

Edmund What?

Eustace Nothing.

Reepicheep What compass bearing?

Eustace East. Due east.

Lucy Oh, no. Not just yet.

The boat runs aground

Reepicheep This, this is where I go on alone. (*He takes off his sword*) I shall need this no more. (*He throws it into the sea*) Goodbye, my friends. I will try to be sad for your sakes. But it has been such a wonderful adventure, and I have only a short way to go to fulfil my true destiny. Even though I am leaving you, believe me, I am truly happy. I know we will meet again, someday. So, until then, brave companions, farewell. Farewell, Queen Lucy.

Lucy hugs him

Reepicheep moves away through the sea of lilies and vanishes

Silence

Eustace That is truly the bravest one of all.

Pause

Edmund Come, Eustace. Come, dear Lucy, don't be sad.

A red glow is visible US

Eustace What's that red glow over there? Not another dragon's cave, I hope.

Edmund I don't know. What do you think, Lucy? Lucy, don't cry . . .

Lucy I'm not crying. I was just wishing and hoping that Reepicheep will have no more fights to fight. And that he will find Aslan.

From the red glow:

Aslan's voice He has already found me. And he has found perfect peace.

Lucy Oh, Aslan, dear Aslan. Is that the way to your country?

Aslan's voice For Reepicheep, but not for you. For you the way into my country lies in your own world.

Edmund What? There's a way from our world?

Aslan's voice Children, there is a way into my country from all the worlds.

Lucy Aslan, will you tell us the way?

Aslan's voice I shall be telling you all the time. But I will not tell you how long or short that way will be. Only that you will have to cross a great river. But do not fear that crossing—for I am the bridge builder. And now come. I will open a door in the sky and send you home to your own land.

Lucy Before we go, will you tell us when we can come back to Narnia again?

Aslan's voice Dearest, you and your brother will never come back to Narnia.

Lucy
Edmund } (*together*) Oh, Aslan!

Aslan's voice You are too old, children, and you must begin to come close to your own world, now.

Lucy It isn't just coming back to Narnia, you know. It's *you*. We shan't meet you in our own world. And how can we live never meeting you there?

Aslan's voice But you shall meet me there, dear one.

Eustace Are—are you there, too, Sir?

Aslan's voice I am there. But there I have another name. You must learn to know me by that name. This was the reason you were brought to Narnia. By knowing me here a little, you may know me better there.

Lucy And is Eustace never to come back, either?

Aslan's voice Child, do you really need to know that? Come, I am opening a door into the sky. (*He tears the sky in half*)

CURTAIN

FURNITURE AND PROPERTY LIST

Only essential items are listed below. Further items can be added at the director's discretion.

PROLOGUE

On stage: Nil

ACT I

SCENE 1

On stage: Nil

SCENE 2

On stage: Nil

Off stage: Flagon of wine and four cups (**Rynelf**)
Blankets (**Rynelf** and **Reepicheep**)

Personal: **Caspian:** sword (required throughout)
Reepicheep: sword (required throughout)

SCENE 3

On stage: Bushes

Off stage: Whip (**Tacks**)
Chair (**Caspian**)

Personal: **Pug** and **Tacks:** bits of string and gags
Bern: horn

SCENE 4

On stage: Nil

SCENE 5

On stage: Coin
Armlet

Personal: **Edmund:** sword (required throughout)

ACT II

Scene 1

On stage: Pool of water

Scene 2

On stage: Nil

Off stage: Spear (**Stage Management**)
Book and lectern (**Stage Management**)

Scene 3

On stage: Nil

Scene 4

On stage: Pillars
Table. *On it:* plates with food, flagon and cups

Off stage: Candlestick (**Daughter**)

Scene 5

On stage: Bucket

LIGHTING PLOT

Practical fittings required: nil
Various simple interior and exterior settings on an open stage

PROLOGUE

To open: Dazzling sun

ACT I

To open: General interior lighting

Cue 1	As the **Children** fight *Reduce lighting*	(Page 5)
Cue 2	To open SCENE 2 *Bring up bright sunlight*	(Page 5)
Cue 3	**Drinian:** "Perhaps . . ." *Black-out*	(Page 9)
Cue 4	To open SCENE 3 *Bring up bright lighting*	(Page 9)
Cue 5	All exit *Reduce lighting*	(Page 16)
Cue 6	To open SCENE 4 *The sky darkens, storm*	(Page 16)
Cue 7	**Drinian:** "SAVE OUR SOULS!" *Black-out*	(Page 17)
Cue 8	To open SCENE 5 *Bring up warm evening light*	(Page 17)
Cue 9	**Drinian:** ". . . to help the poor boy." *Dim lights. Full moon*	(Page 20)
Cue 10	**Reepicheep:** ". . . our trust in Aslan!" *Black-out*	(Page 23)

ACT II

To open: Golden, hazy lighting

Cue 11	To open SCENE 2 *Cross fade to dull white lighting*	(Page 26)

Cue 12	The upstairs of the house comes into view	(Page 30)
	Cross fade to eerie interior lighting	

Cue 13	The wind rises	(Page 34)
	Black-out	

Cue 14	To open SCENE 3	(Page 34)
	Bring up bright lighting	

Cue 15 **Eustace:** "... into terrible trouble, Reep."   (Page 35)
Reduce lighting

Cue 16 **Caspian:** "Battle stations, everyone."   (Page 35)
Black-out

Cue 17 **Rynelf:** "Light! Light ahead."   (Page 36)
Searchlight beam hits Dawn Treader

Cue 18 **Caspian:** "... to the last three noble Lords."   (Page 36)
Bring up pale blue lighting

Cue 19 A door opens   (Page 37)
Back light door for silhouette effect

Cue 20 **Daughter:** "Look!" (She points to the doorway)   (Page 38)
Bring up dawn effect

Cue 21 **Ramandu** and his **Daughter** start singing   (Page 38)
Cross fade to warm bright lighting

Cue 22 **Edmund:** "... dear Lucy, don't be sad."   (Page 43)
Snap on red spot on US

PROJECTION PLOT

ACT I

SCENE 1

Cue 1   When ready   (Page 3)
Bring up dragon-ship projection on wall US

Cue 2   They turn away   (Page 4)
Gradually enlarge dragon-ship projection

Cue 3   As they struggle   (Page 5)
Further enlarge dragon-ship projection

Cue 4   As the **Children** fall into the sea   (Page 5)
Fade dragon-ship projection

SCENE 5

Cue 5   The **Dragon** withdraws into the cave   (Page 21)
After a pause, bring up projection of dragon flying across the moon

ACT II

SCENE 1

Cue 6   **Lucy:** "... he'd stop you fighting ... ooh!"   (Page 26)
Projection of **Aslan** *on wall* US, *fade after a few moments*

SCENE 2

Cue 7   **Lucy:** "I must say that spell."   (Page 30)
Bring up projection of **Aslan** *on wall* US, *then fade after roar*

Cue 8   **Lucy:** "... my two schoolfriends, Marjorie Preston and Anne Featherstone."   (Page 31)
Bring up projection of two girls sitting in a train compartment

Cue 9   **Lucy:** "... you two-faced beast."   (Page 31)
Fade train compartment projection

EFFECTS PLOT

PROLOGUE

Cue 1	When ready *Sounds of crowd*	(Page 1)
Cue 2	**Miraz:** "... what I like with Narnia." *Roar of a lion*	(Page 1)

ACT I

Cue 3	As the **Children** struggle *Sound of waves, wind and gulls*	(Page 5)
Cue 4	**Eustace:** "Save me! Save me!" *Cut sound of waves, wind and gulls*	(Page 5)
Cue 5	The slave train comes on *A bell begins to toll*	(Page 14)
Cue 6	**Gumpas:** "Pug, pray continue." *Cut bell*	(Page 14)
Cue 7	**Caspian** blows the horn *Sound of horn, followed by sounds of answering horns, cheering, firecrackers, off*	(Page 15)
Cue 8	**Reepicheep:** "... the utter East." *Wind stirs*	(Page 16)
Cue 9	**Reepicheep:** "... true adventure really starts!" *Increase wind effect*	(Page 16)
Cue 10	All exit *The wind rises to a full hurricane*	(Page 16)
Cue 11	**Drinian:** "SAVE OUR SOULS!" *Splintering noise*	(Page 17)
Cue 12	**Eustace:** "What's that over there?" *Jets of smoke from* US	(Page 17)
Cue 13	**Drinian:** "What's the matter?" *Twin jets of smoke from* US	(Page 18)
Cue 14	The silhouette of a dragon flies across the moon *Roar of a lion and terrible screams*	(Page 21)
Cue 15	**Reepicheep:** "... put our trust in Aslan!" *Roar of a lion*	(Page 21)

ACT II

MADE AND PRINTED IN GREAT BRITAIN BY
LATIMER TREND & COMPANY LTD PLYMOUTH

MADE IN ENGLAND

Act 1 De 5

p 30 & 31